In Mexico graffiti is
a subject of which we all have
something to say, no doubt
we have seen many adorning
or dirtying our urban environment
as clearly the point of view
of each individual.

This time the author speaks to us
of this topic, addressing it from the
Simpler and more possible way.

Whether you like graffiti or not, without
doubt this guide will be useful for
know more about this
urbanized world.

In matters of graffiti the accessory
more common to make a piece, bomb, tag
or character (drawings on wall) is the spray,
since with that you can do that kind of work.

Some graffiti artists feel free to experience
and create very varied pieces due to the wide manageability
That has the spray.

After using it well you can solve any challenge that
Present in a drawing.

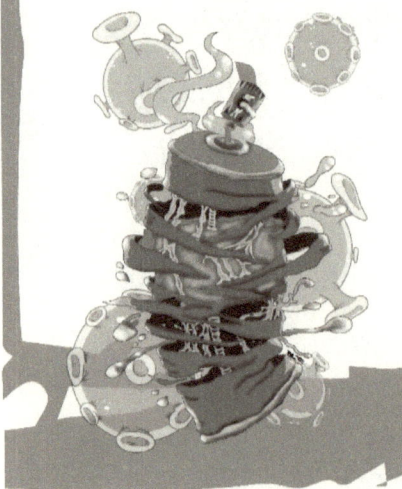

More expensive

Masks in graffiti are a very common instrument, since that with these we can take care of pollution to ourselves. Some sprays can affect our organism, they are very good when large pieces are made but in reality they should be used in any circumstances.

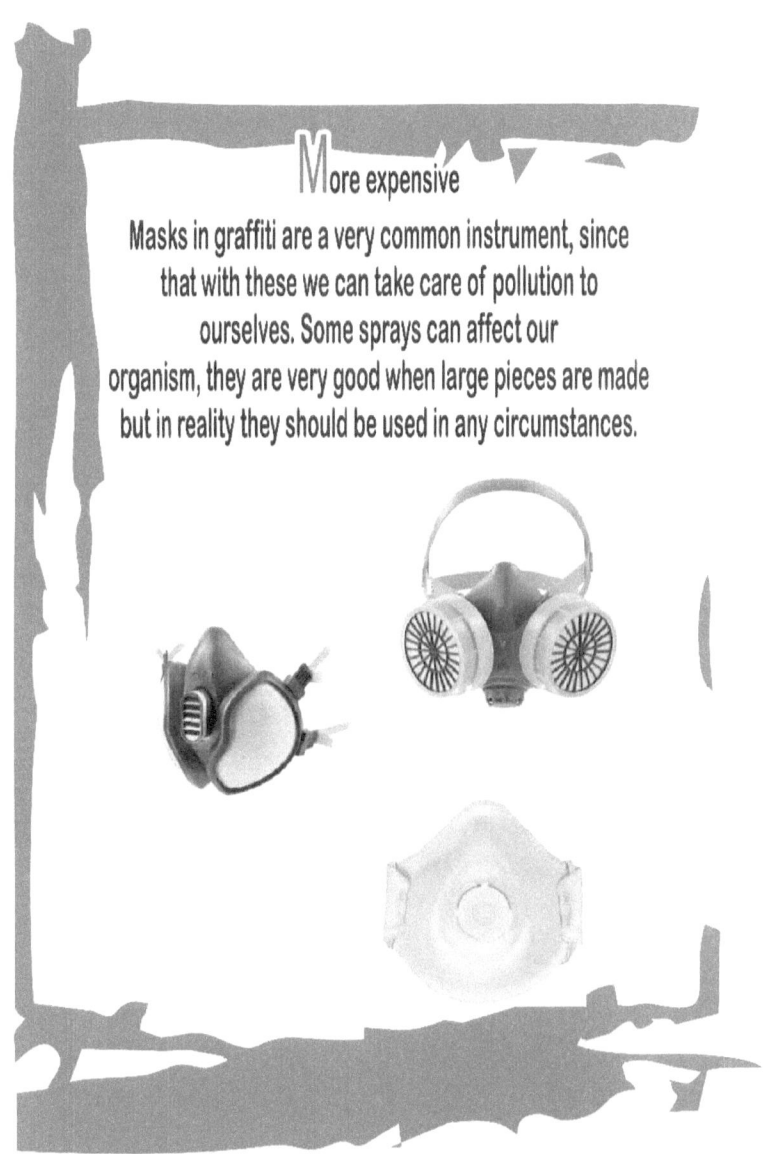

Feathers

In the middle of graffiti the use of the pen is very common, since
either to ink some sketch or to draw it from
Zero with that material. Perhaps it may seem somewhat crude, because
It is a material without artistic qualities; however can
Be quite comfortable.

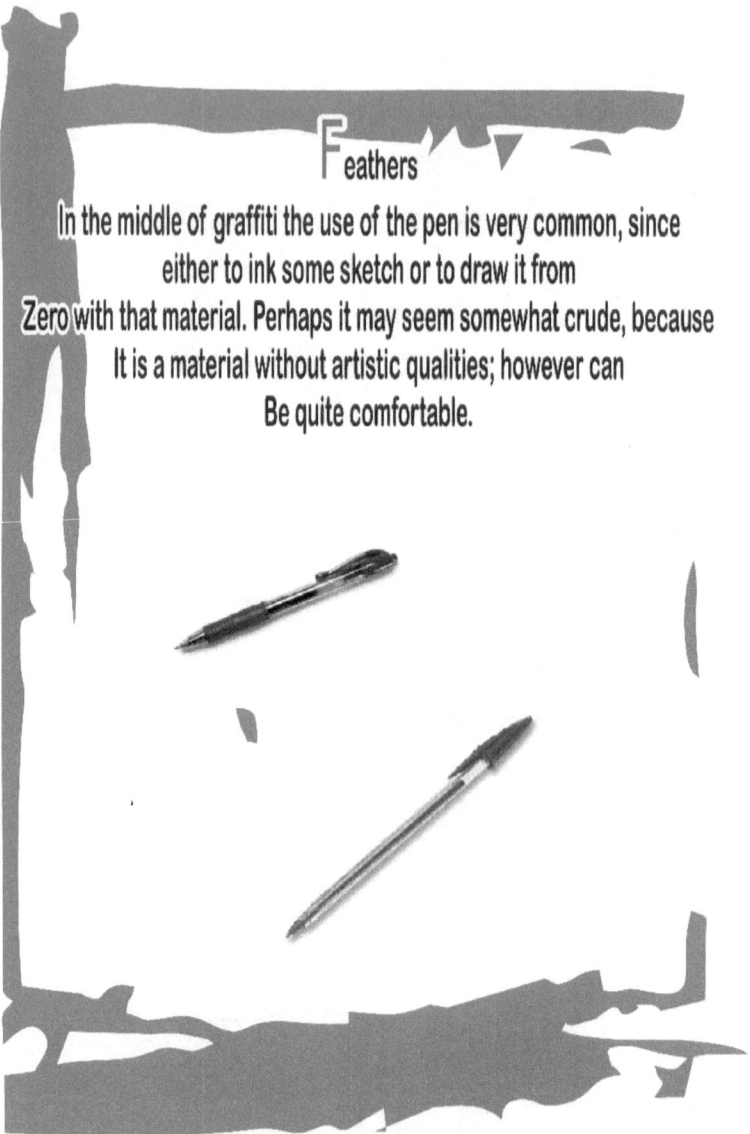

Airbrush

The airbrush is another instrument widely used by
graffiti artists, since it equals or at least looks as if
it was graffiti with spray in one more way
comfortable and compact, so to speak is an emulator of
canned spray There are several models and types of airbrushes
from the professional to the beginner, of different
costs and manageability.

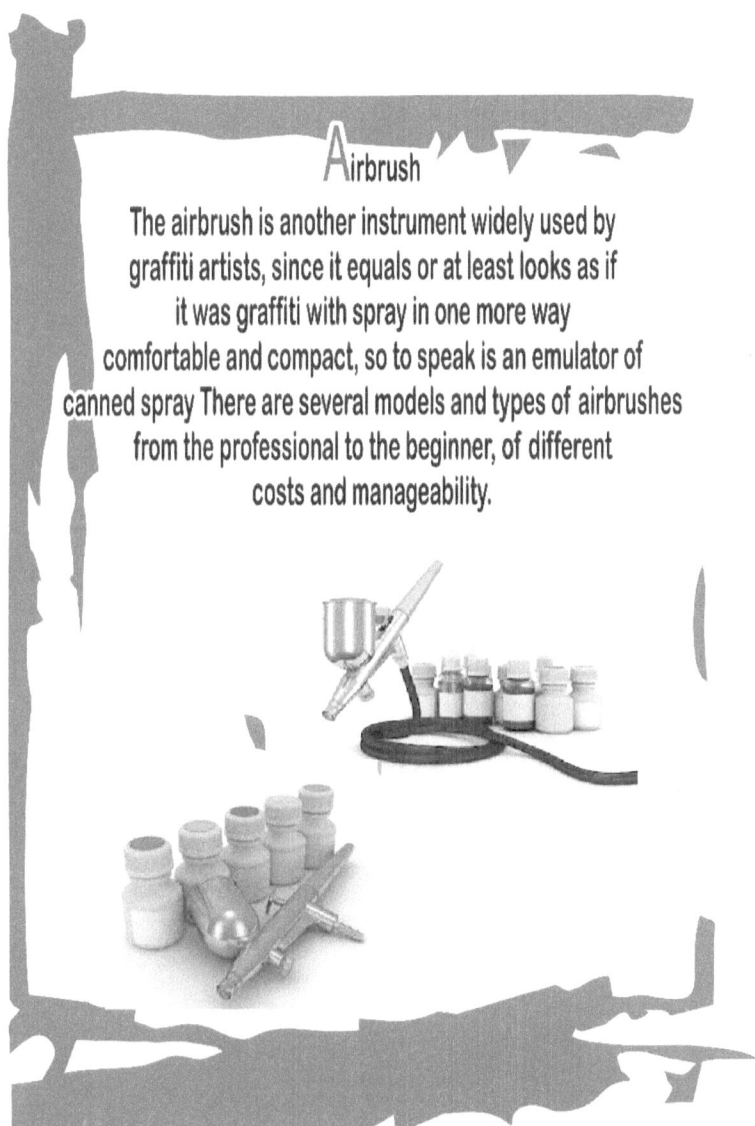

Markers

These are very practical. With them the graffiti artists
beginners are dedicated to tagging (Signing).
For this they go through the streets and paint in walls, booths
telephone and other surfaces.
Fat and chubby markers of various brands
they are very common among graffiti artists, in addition to
train the handling of thick lines.

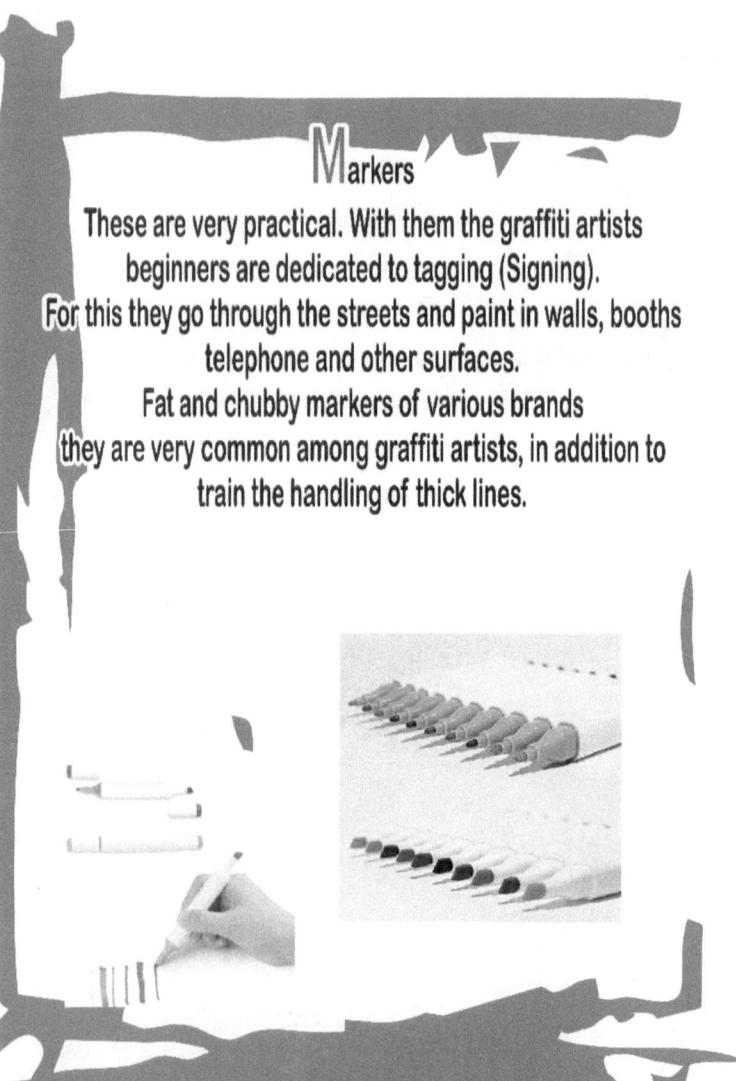

Pencils

Pencils are very helpful when drawing or
tracing letters is about; they are an indispensable instrument to the
Time to create any idea on paper. All kinds of drawings
and letters can be defined with this instrument. Search different
pencil qualities, those with the letter H are harder
(greater dark tone) and those of the B are softer (smaller
saturation).

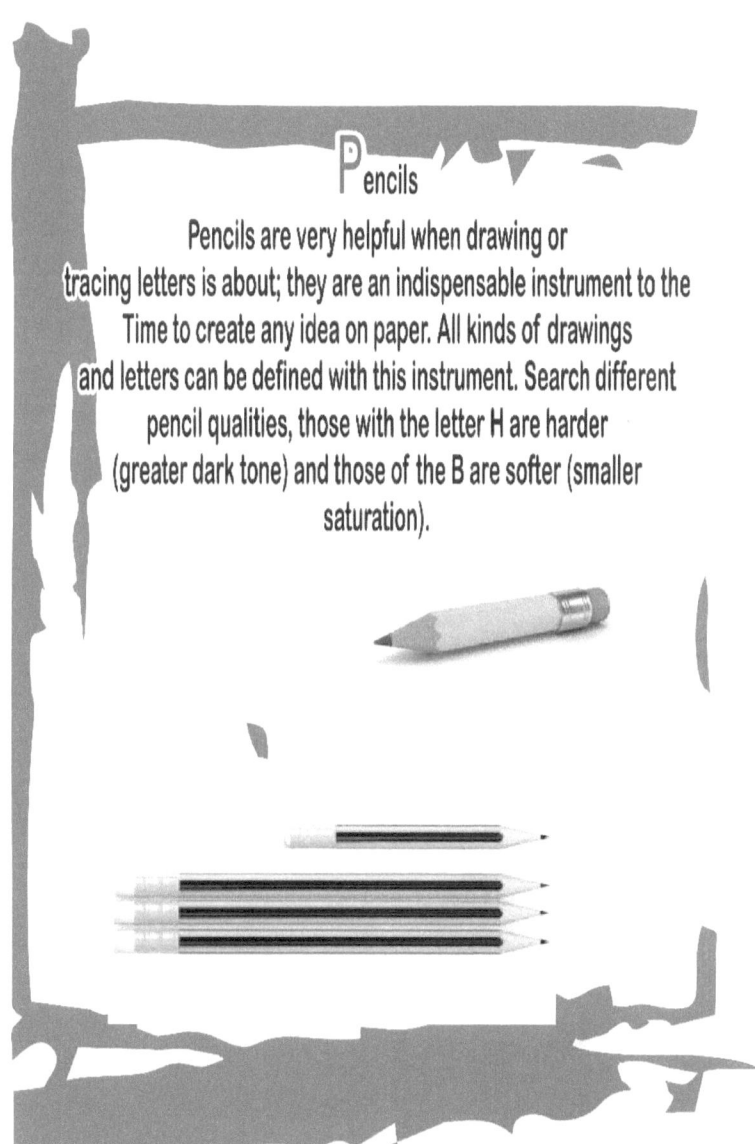

Black Book

Graffiti artists call it obviously because of its appearance.
They find their bombs (jobs that have
done in your free time or even professionally).
It can also be called gallery graff (graffiti gallery),
since there are exposed his most recognizable sketches made
Of course for themselves.

Caps or Valves.

Here we have a great variety of valves, which serve for each type of work, to make the biggest tip or as pen type very thin and delineated. The most common are: "Fat Cap, Calligraphic, Punto Rosa, Punta Blanca, the Australian."

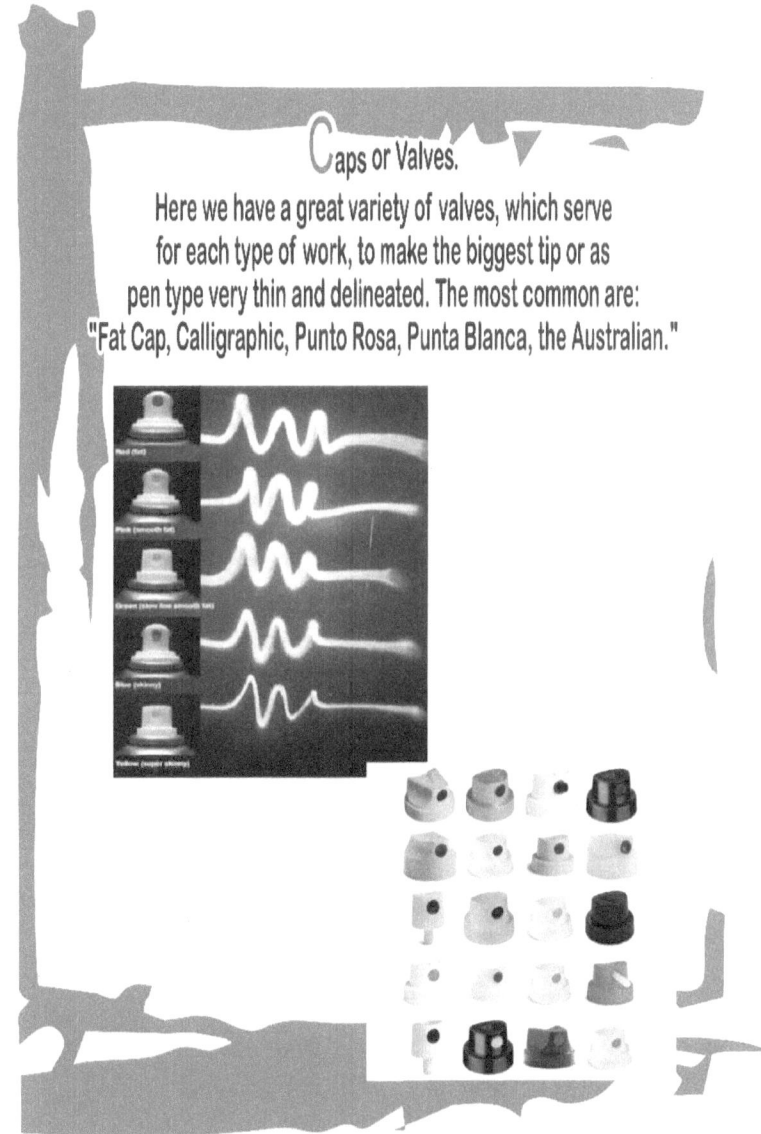

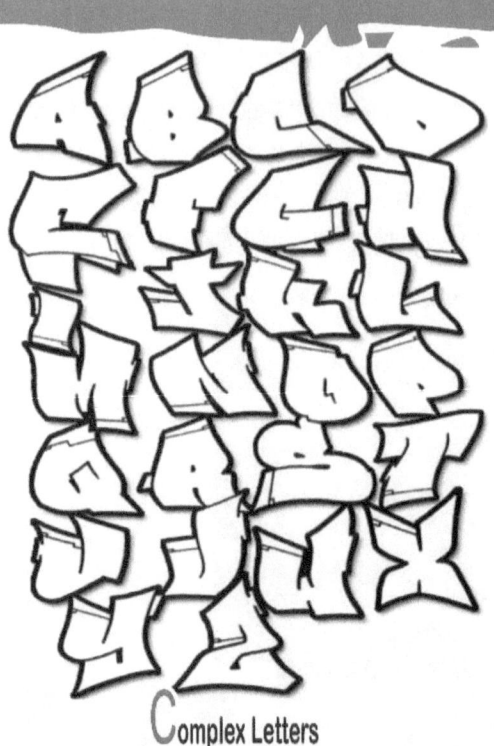

Complex Letters

This is a more complex case. Make this type of letters
on the wall or on any surface it is difficult, but
not impossible. From here you start to start making lyrics
with arrows that sometimes do not reach
Understand what they say.

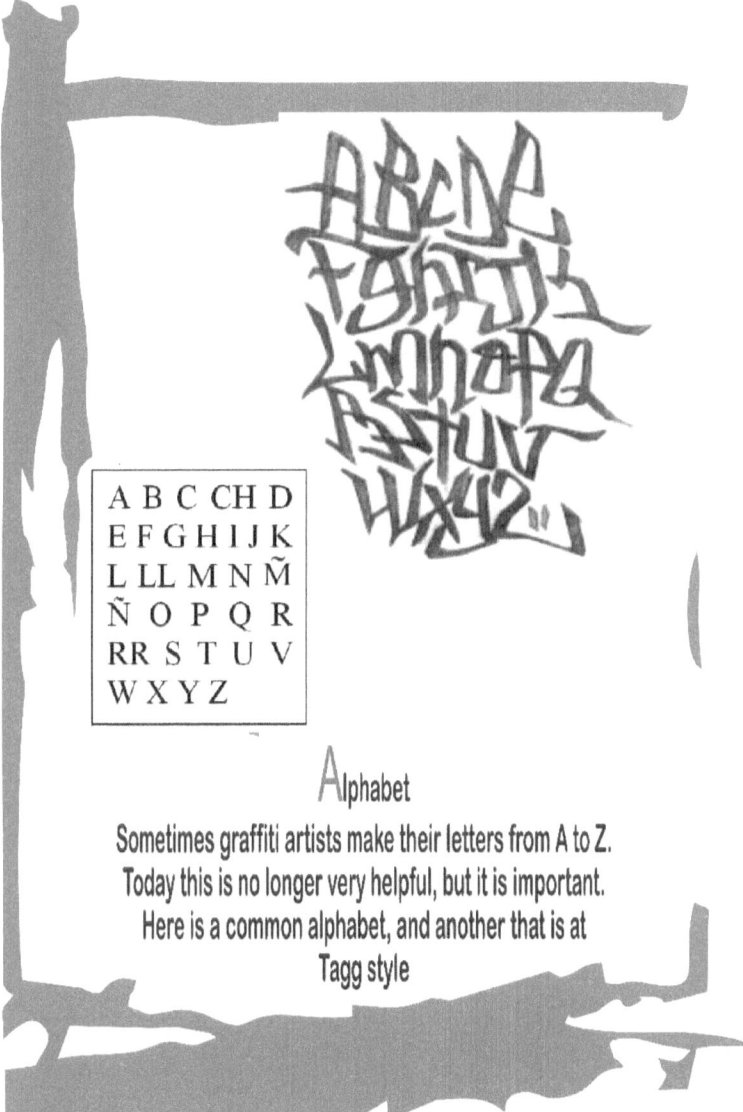

A	B	C	CH	D
E	F	G	H	I J	K
L	LL	M	N	M̃
Ñ	O	P	Q	R
RR	S	T	U	V
W	X	Y	Z	

Alphabet

Sometimes graffiti artists make their letters from A to Z.
Today this is no longer very helpful, but it is important.
Here is a common alphabet, and another that is at
Tagg style

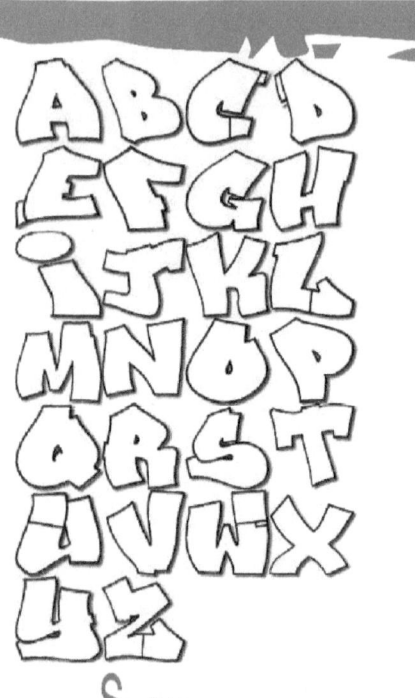

Straight pumps

This is a bomb style alphabet. Obviously it's called that
by its inflated shape. It is very common to see lyrics how are you in
walls or in a black book. Here I leave you this alphabet
To take advantage of it.

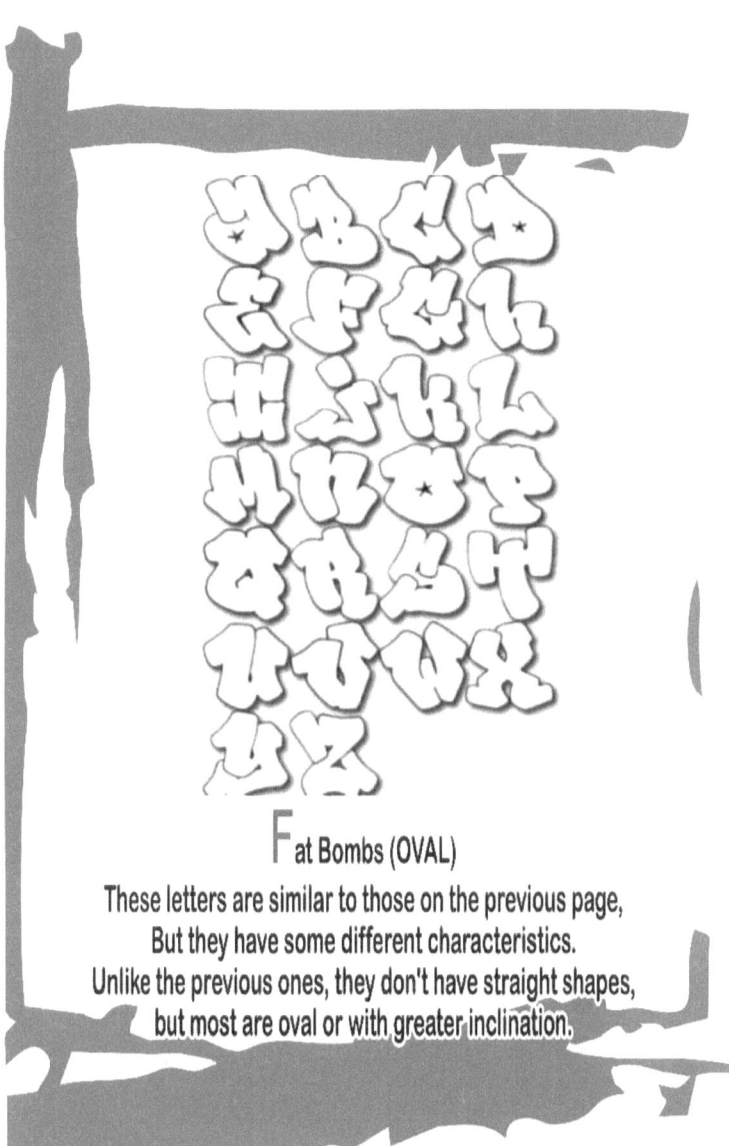

F at Bombs (OVAL)

These letters are similar to those on the previous page,
But they have some different characteristics.
Unlike the previous ones, they don't have straight shapes,
but most are oval or with greater inclination.

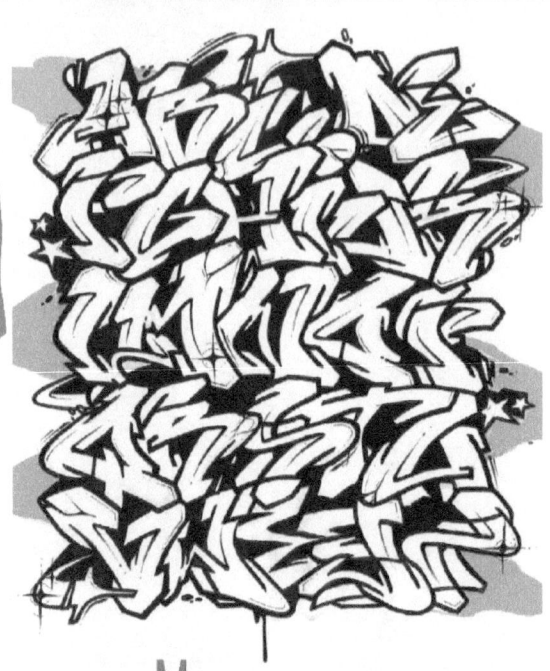

More Elaborate Letters

Here we find a more complex alphabet than the
previous, since there are endless details.
Before drawing these types of letters, it is important to draw
Well, the ones that are simpler.

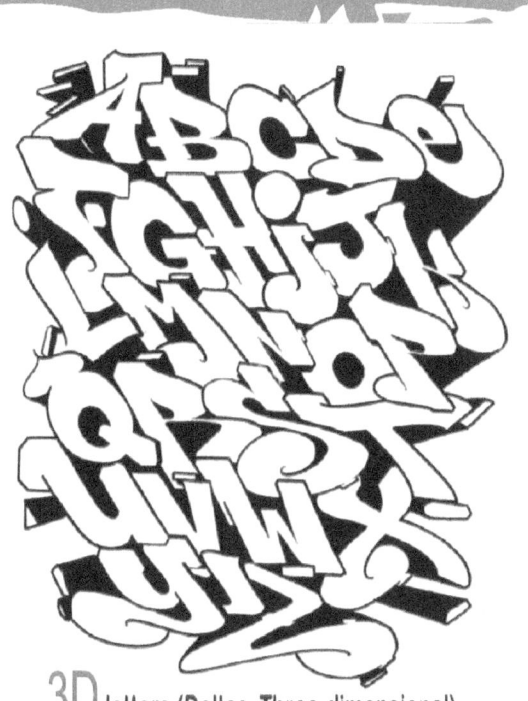

—3D letters (Deltas, Three-dimensional)

This type of lyrics is even more complex than the previous ones. When we start painting graffiti we will draw more or less letters sensillas, but little by little we should look for more complexity in this case we will call them 3D letters, since if they check well they seem to stand out from the paper, and colored look better.

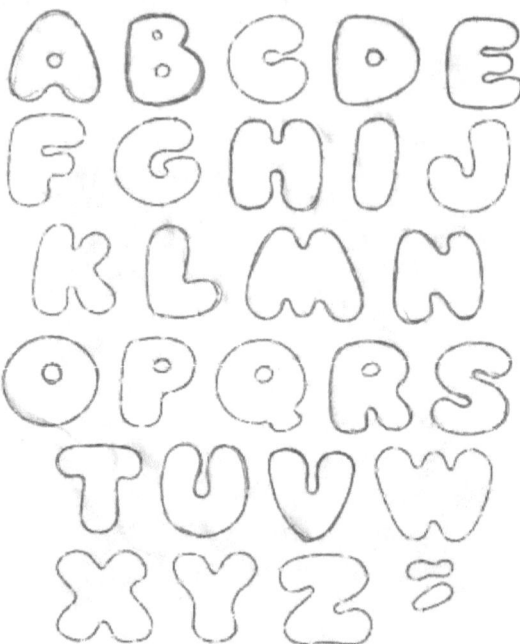

As you can see, here we have straight oval letters, with larger straight sections

But most of it is oval.

These letters are simple to make and we trace them in Three slightly different styles.

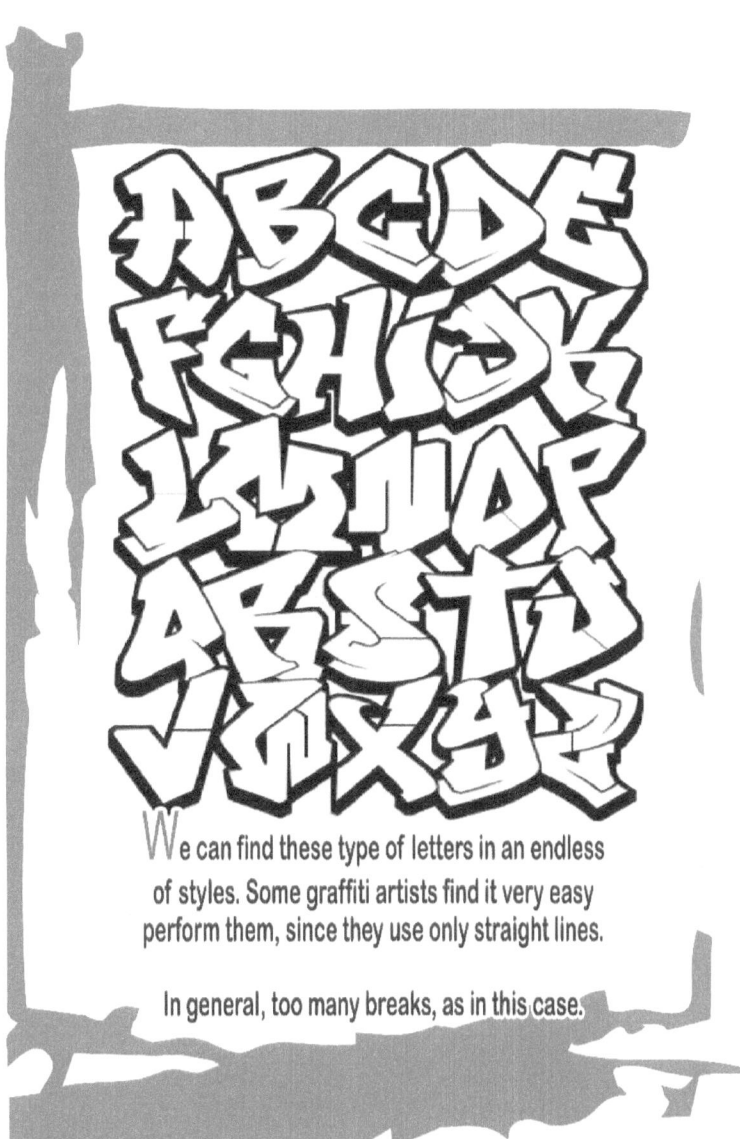

We can find these type of letters in an endless of styles. Some graffiti artists find it very easy perform them, since they use only straight lines.

In general, too many breaks, as in this case.

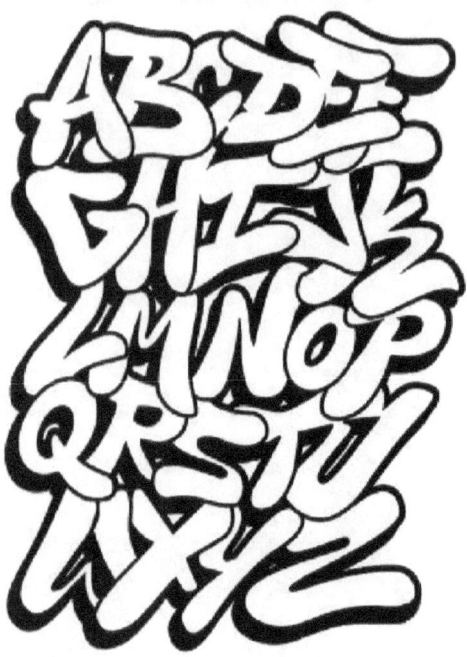

Oval letters

This type of lyrics is the simplest thing there is. Basically
all are resolved based on circle or circle means.

Usually, these type of letters give an opposite impression
to the aggressiveness of straight lines.

18

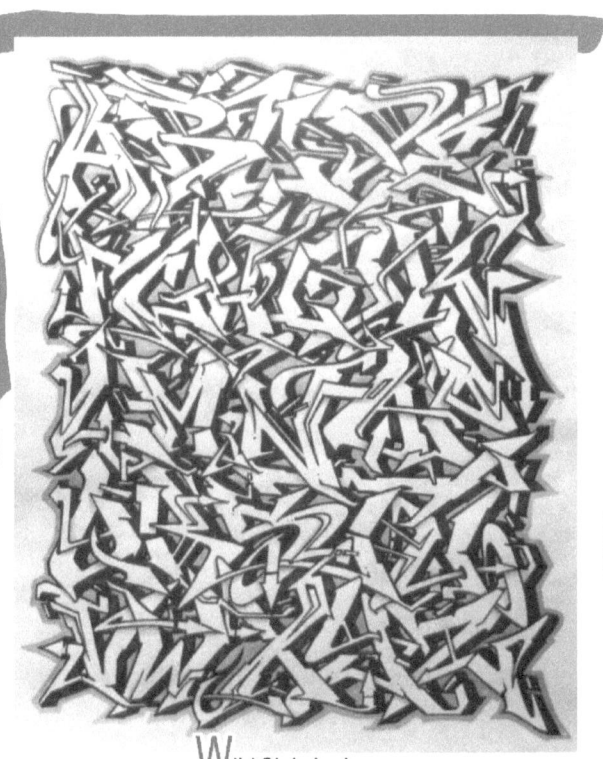

Wild Style Lyrics

The wild style lyrics today are very helpful, since
in the Old School (old school) letters like
these that were understood with relative ease.
The opposite case are those that only seek
the most aesthetic and exaggerated way, without trying
Give a particular message or word.

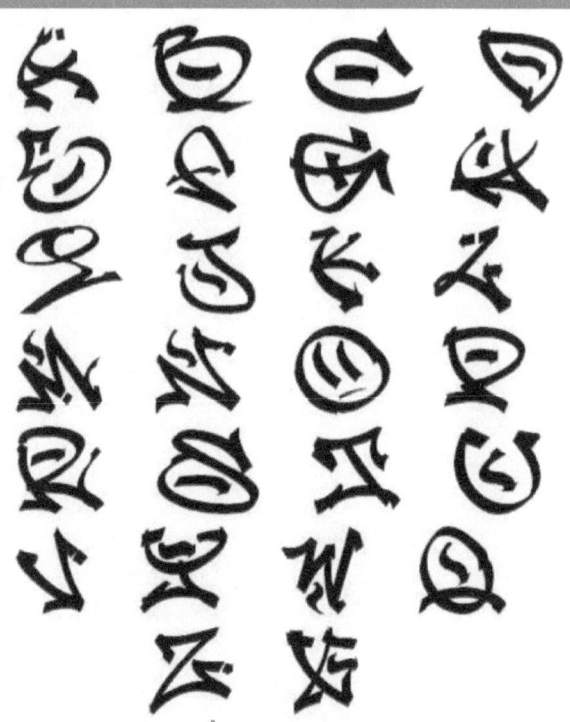

Letters Taggs 2

As we said before, taggs are very difficult to understand.
Here is another example.
They are also usually unified by a single stroke,
or placed on top of each other.

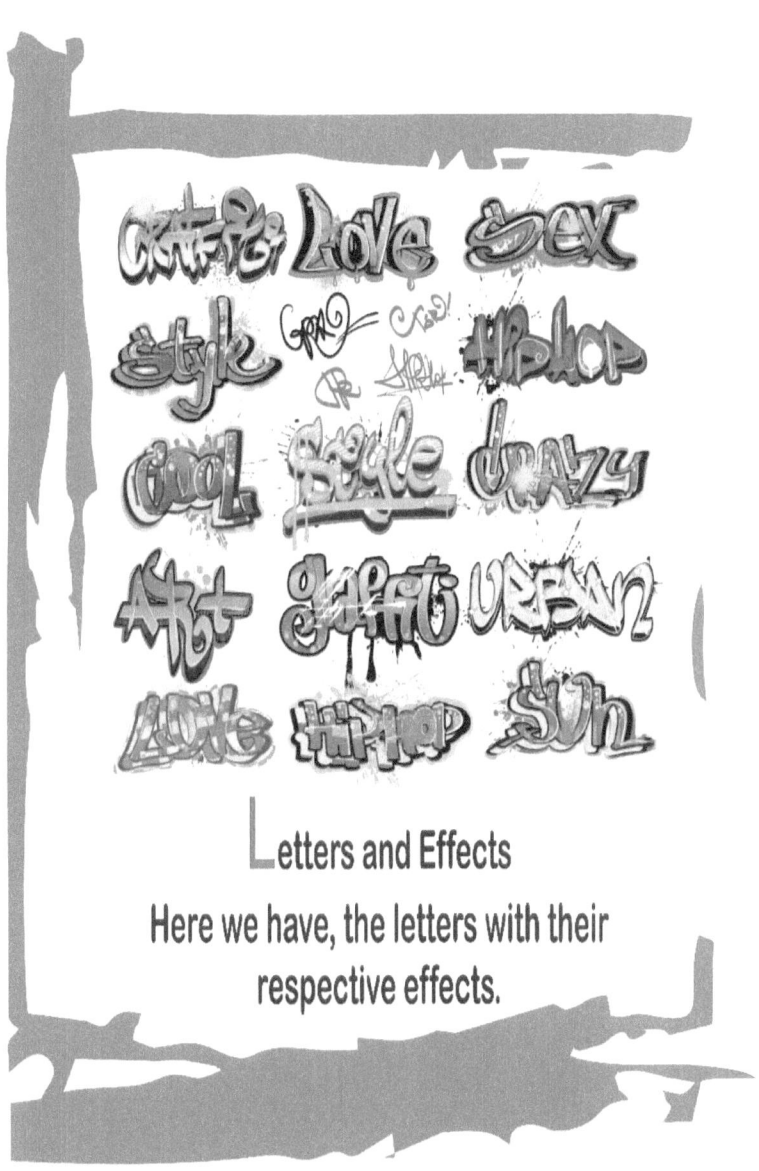

Letters and Effects

Here we have, the letters with their respective effects.

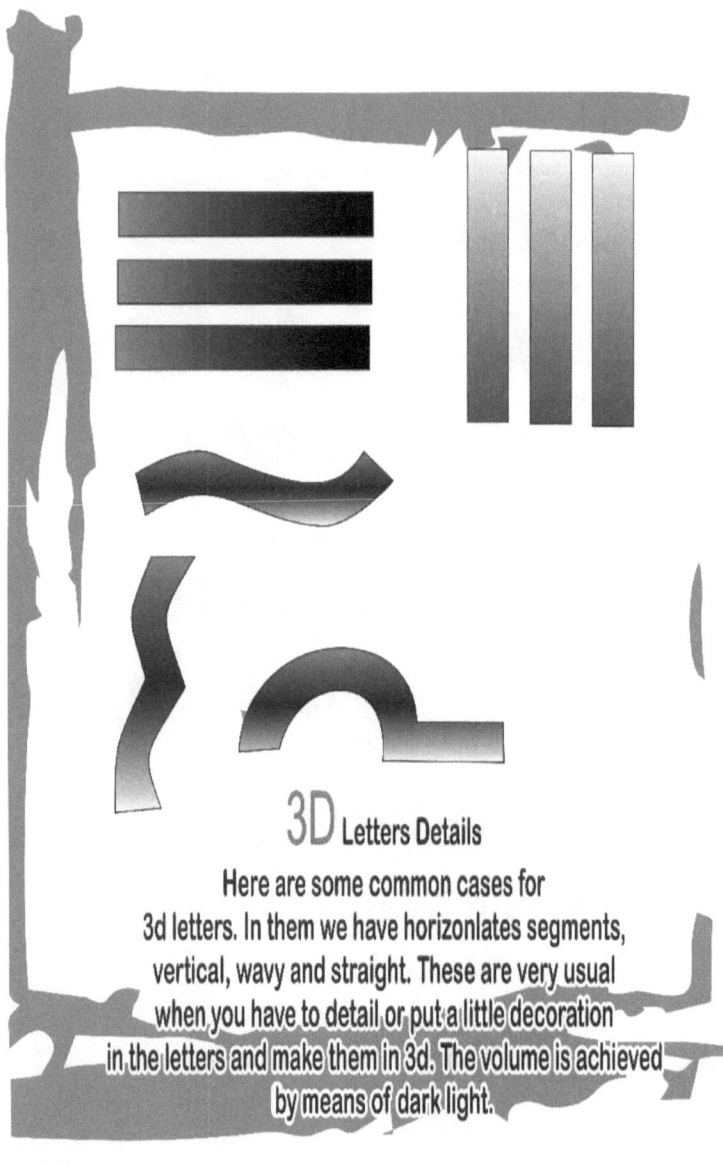

3D Letters Details

Here are some common cases for
3d letters. In them we have horizonlates segments,
vertical, wavy and straight. These are very usual
when you have to detail or put a little decoration
in the letters and make them in 3d. The volume is achieved
by means of dark light.

ABCDE
FGHIJ
KLMNO
PQRST
UVWXY
Z

Taggs lyrics

Here we have a particular case. It's about the ways
that we call "Taggs", because they are a kind
of hieroglyph that are not understood with the naked eye.

In some cases they are more readable while in most
do not.
Understanding this, it's about understanding the best
Possibly what they really say.

23

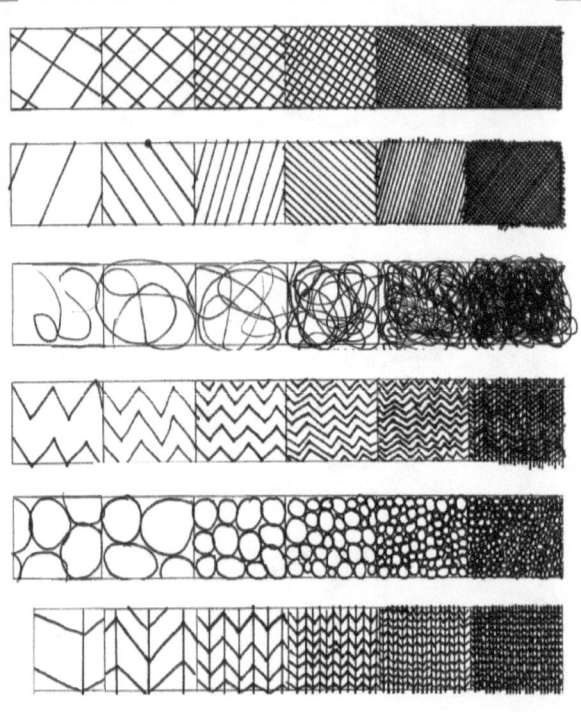

Also in this case we use the most practical when
we draw, this is the "Ashurado" and the gradient that we
they serve to make the letters we want to see in
Third dimension. For this it is necessary that you study
The theme about light and shadow.

A B C D E F G
H I J K L M N
O P Q R S T U
V W X Y Z

Simple Letters without Effect

Here we have some letters. To do this job
let's see that it is a simple path as seen in
"Taggs 1 and 2" in this case can be performed
of different colors or on top of each other
they can also be used as a base for better effects
and finishes.

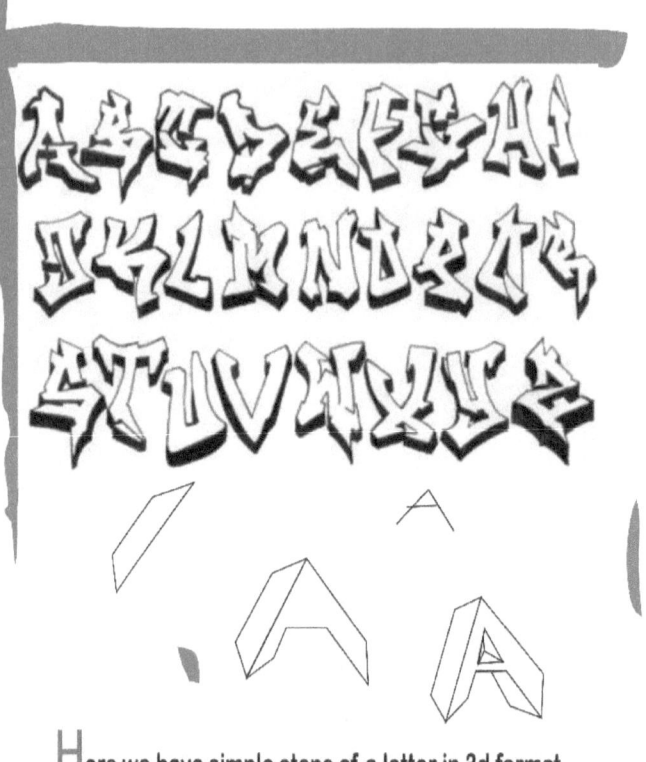

Here we have simple steps of a letter in 3d format.
As you can see it is not difficult, but if we want and try
to make it more complex, we can perform
something extraordinary
Starting with something more basic.

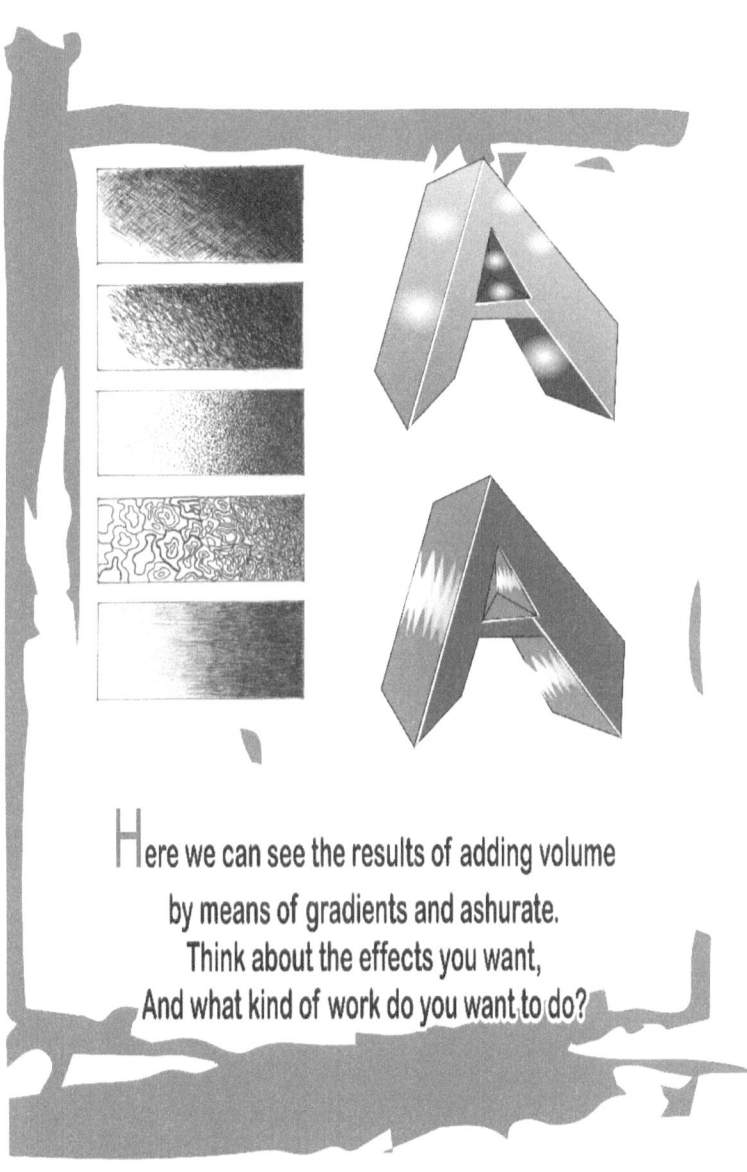

Here we can see the results of adding volume
by means of gradients and ashurate.
Think about the effects you want,
And what kind of work do you want to do?

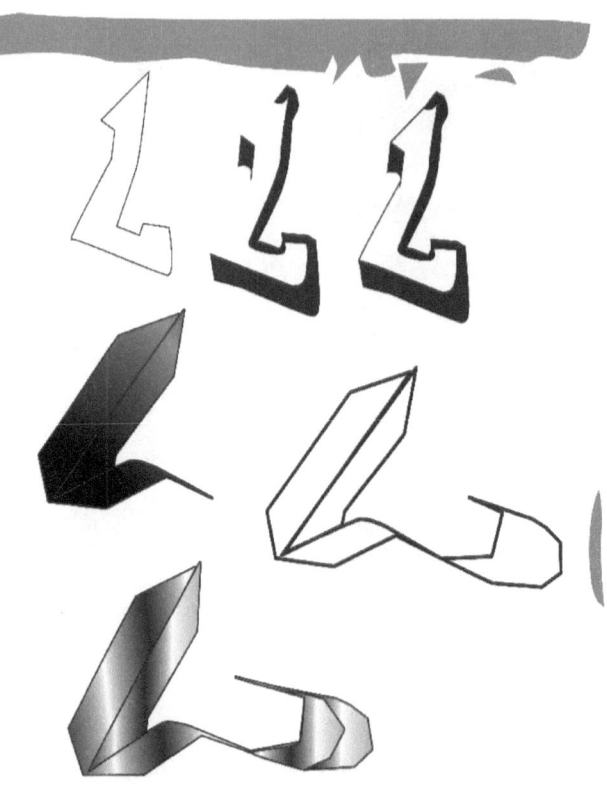

Here we have the letter L step by step, but it has a detail, these are vertical lines, some of which we saw earlier, that they merely decorate Our alphabet.

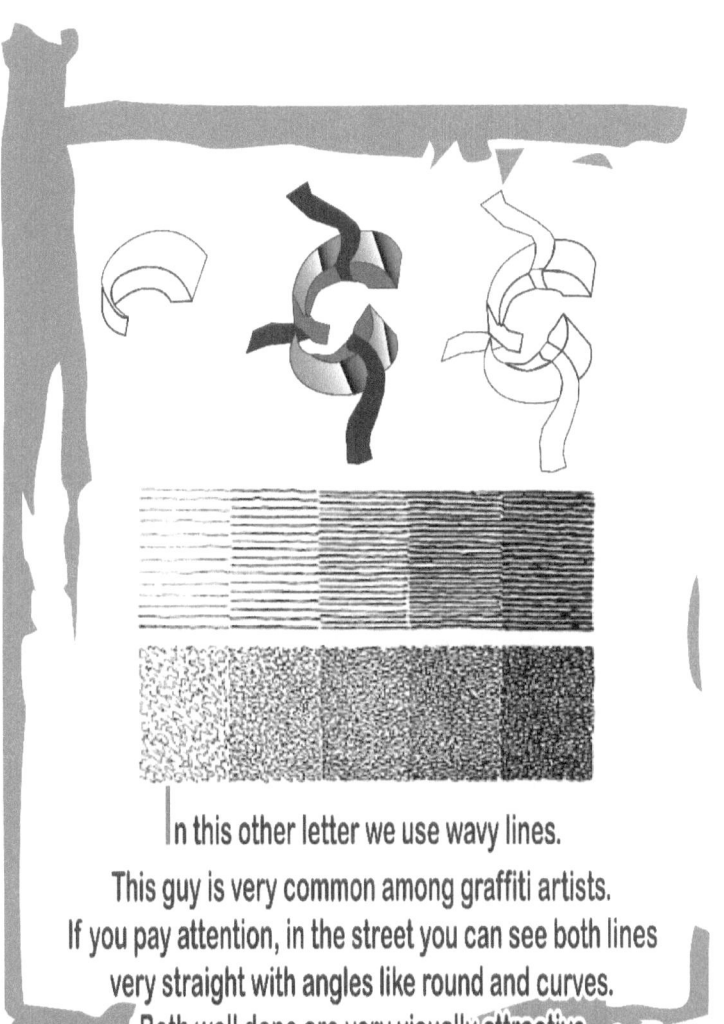

In this other letter we use wavy lines.

This guy is very common among graffiti artists.
If you pay attention, in the street you can see both lines
very straight with angles like round and curves.
Both well done are very visually attractive
In addition to the gradient finish.

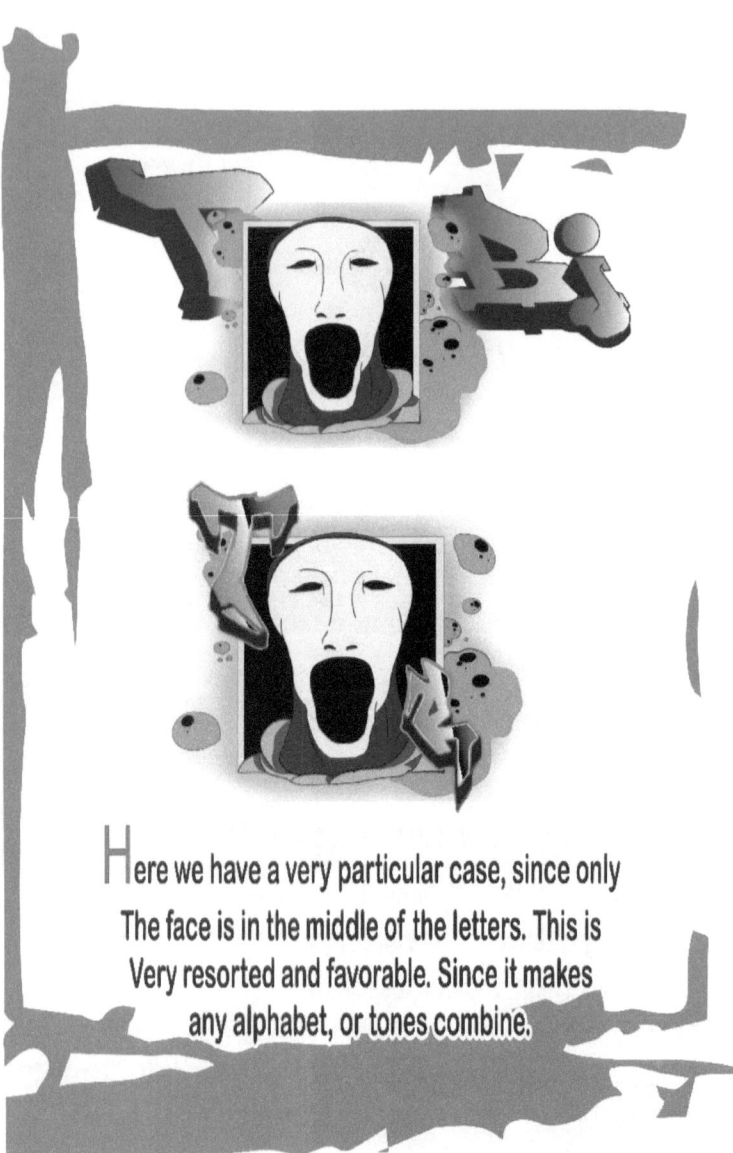

Here we have a very particular case, since only
The face is in the middle of the letters. This is
Very resorted and favorable. Since it makes
any alphabet, or tones combine.

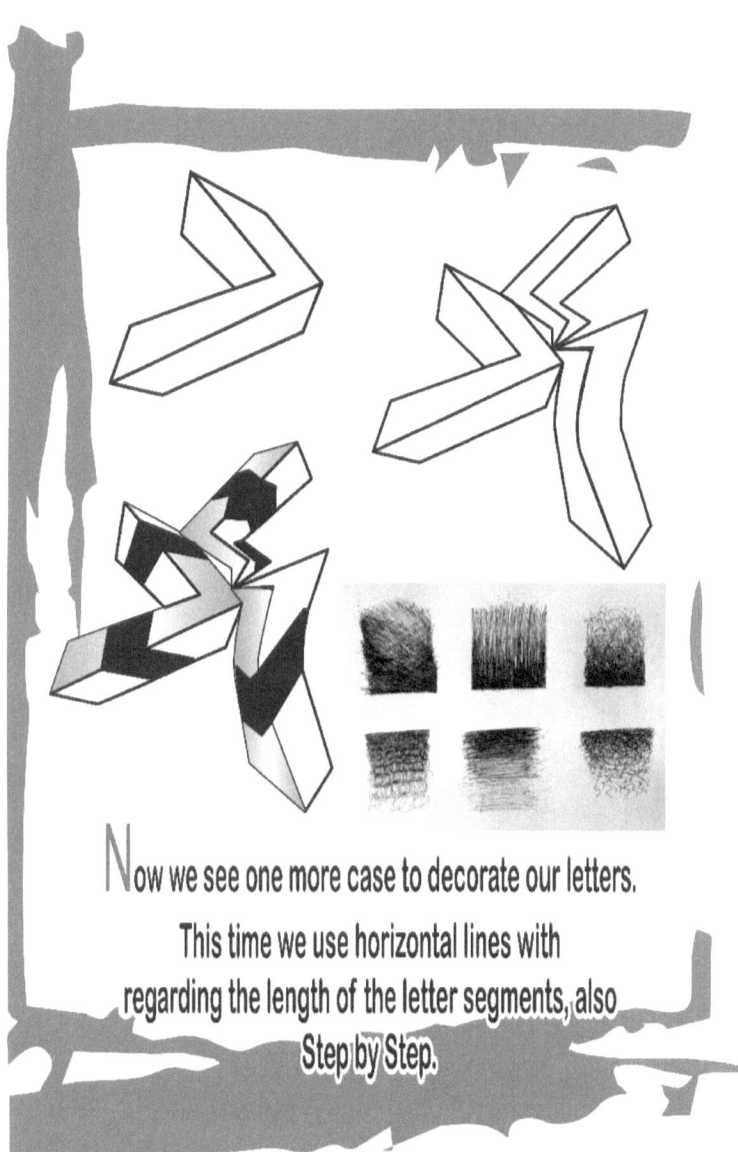

Now we see one more case to decorate our letters. This time we use horizontal lines with regarding the length of the letter segments, also Step by Step.

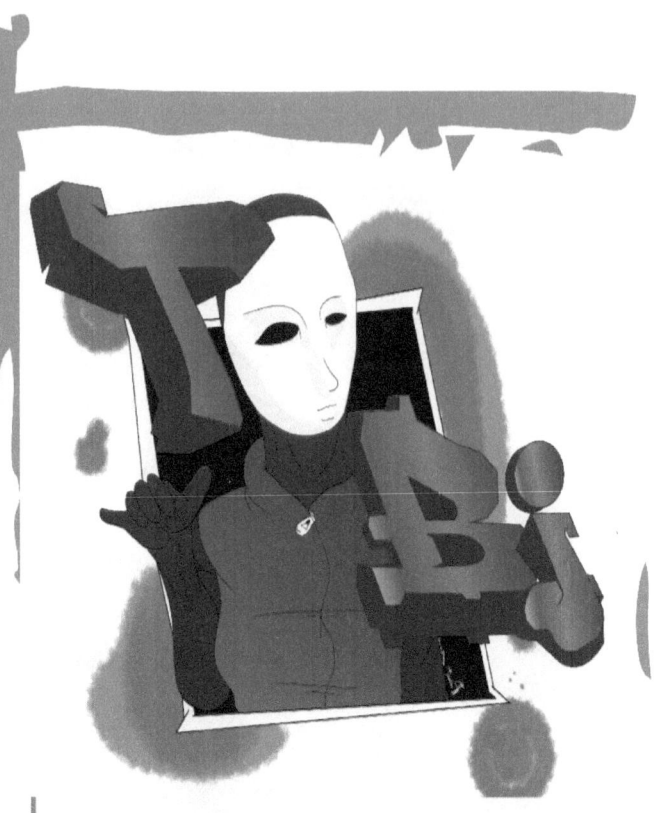

In the final step, the appearance is already defined.
It is very common to see this type of work in the
graffiti artists from practically everyone.
Of course, each one is defined with their personal style.

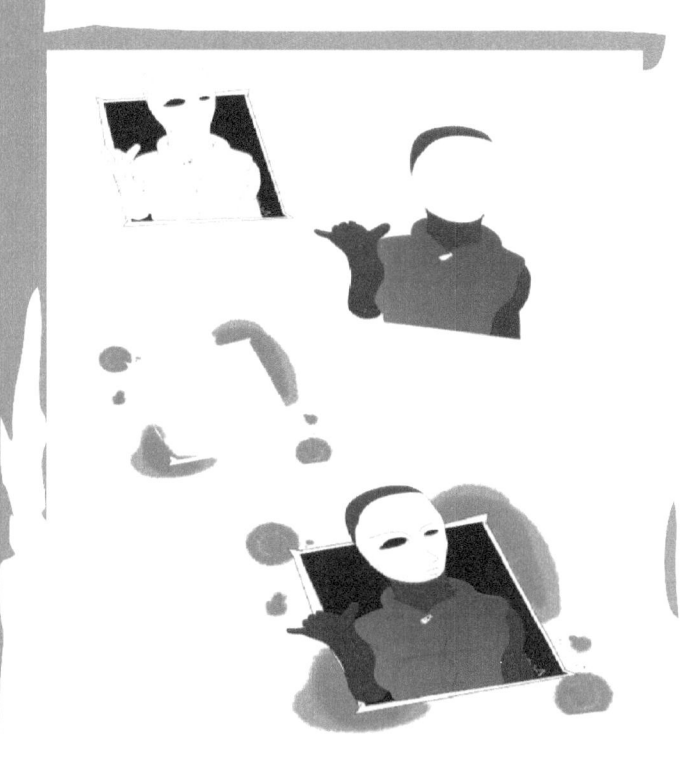

This is another style of composition.
As in traditional drawing, we start with a
outline in basic strokes and then define
and using the color black and go shaping, and volume.

33

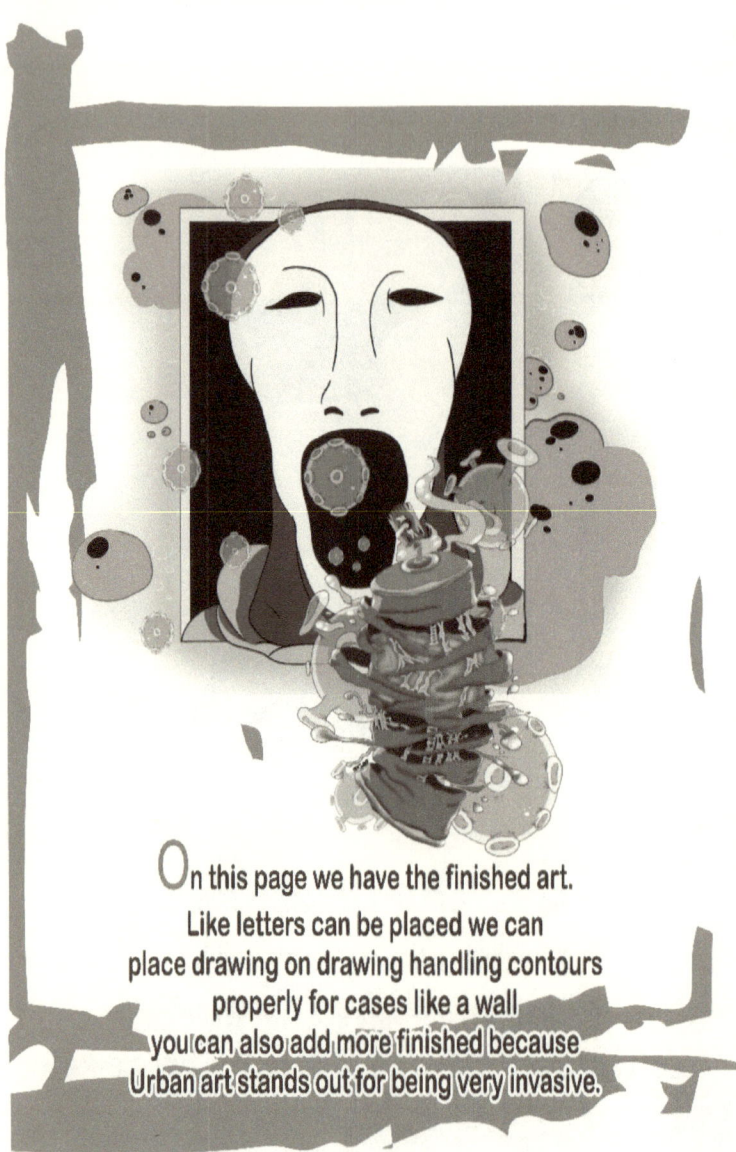

On this page we have the finished art.
Like letters can be placed we can
place drawing on drawing handling contours
properly for cases like a wall
you can also add more finished because
Urban art stands out for being very invasive.

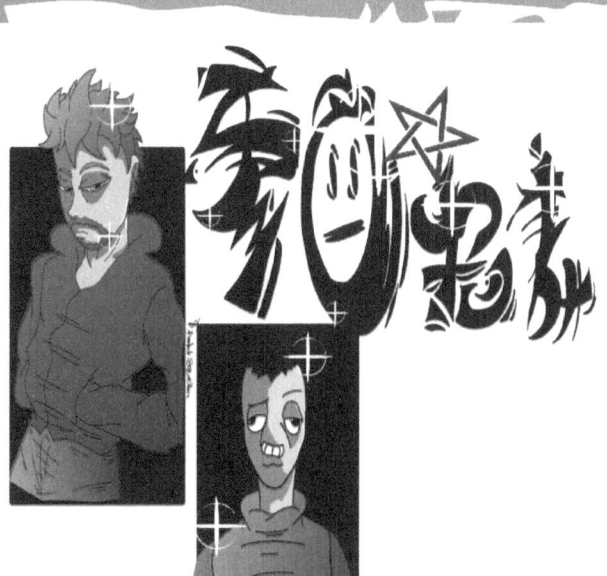

On this page we have an example of how to they made some Wild Style lyrics with certain oriental theme using black as major invasive. Figurative elements the characters left supporting to do more interesting the drawing in general.

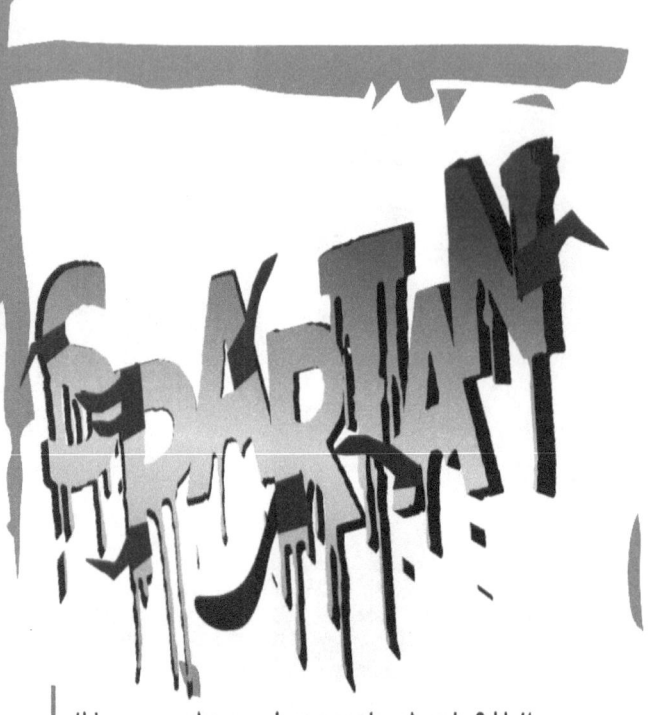

In this case we have a plaque or signature in 3d letters.
already finished with the set, you can do
use of the five elements: Straight, Wavy Lines,
Horizontal, Vertical, and Crossed. This for
create great works in this case has been very simple
but it can have a much more amazing finish.
The finish is gradient based. Some more like it
the classic ashurate, but it is a matter of tastes and styles.

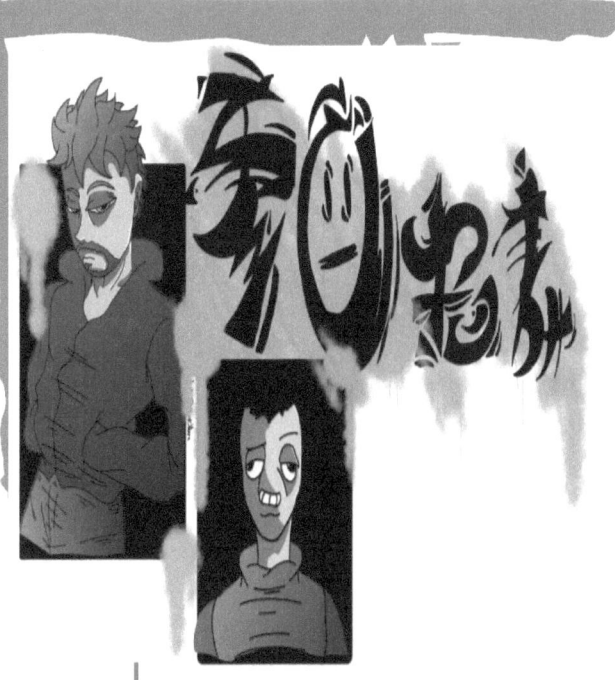

In this part an airbrush effect was used
seemingly messy way but it's
to give a sober, very street urban effect,
as well as a certain lightness of the text,
added to the characters that now happen to have a strength
even more mysterious and even dangerous than in previous pages.

37

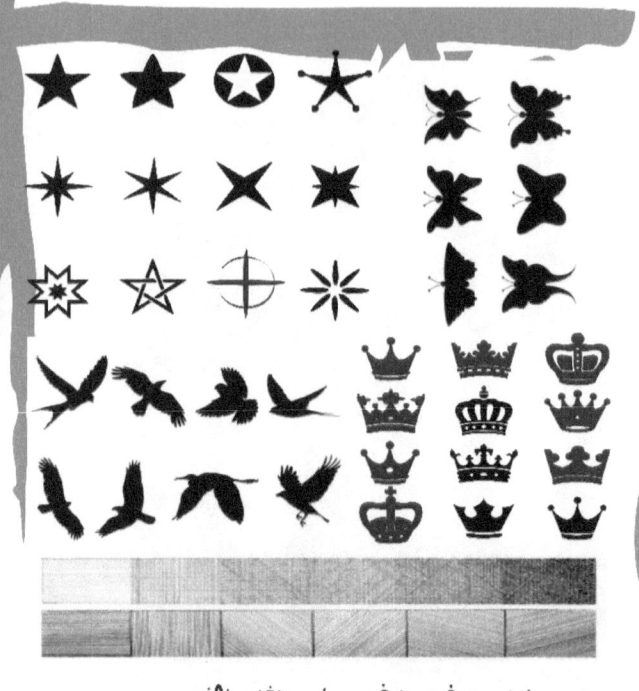

On this page we find examples
of decoration and creation to decorate your letters.
From simple fonts to the most elaborate.
The interesting thing is your ability to adapt these elements
to your graffiti.

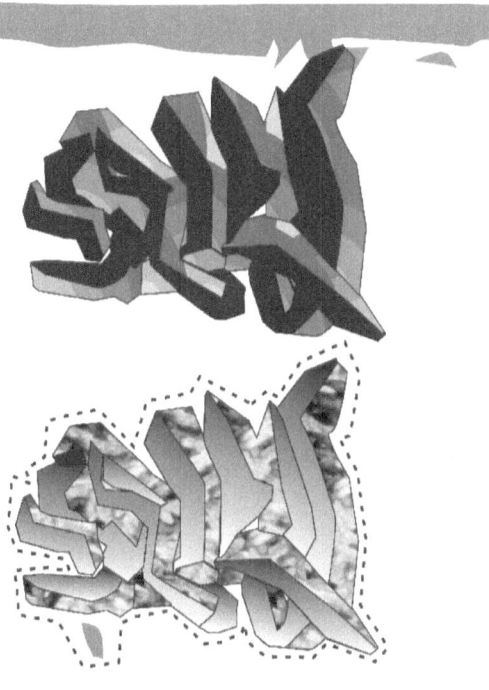

Here we have a gallery made of 3d letters.
If you notice, they are different from each other.
It is logical if you consider that there are an infinity of letters
What you can create If you think about it a bit, really though
Try to copy someone's style
in particular, no matter how hard you try to make it identical, some of
Your style will certainly be printed in your work.

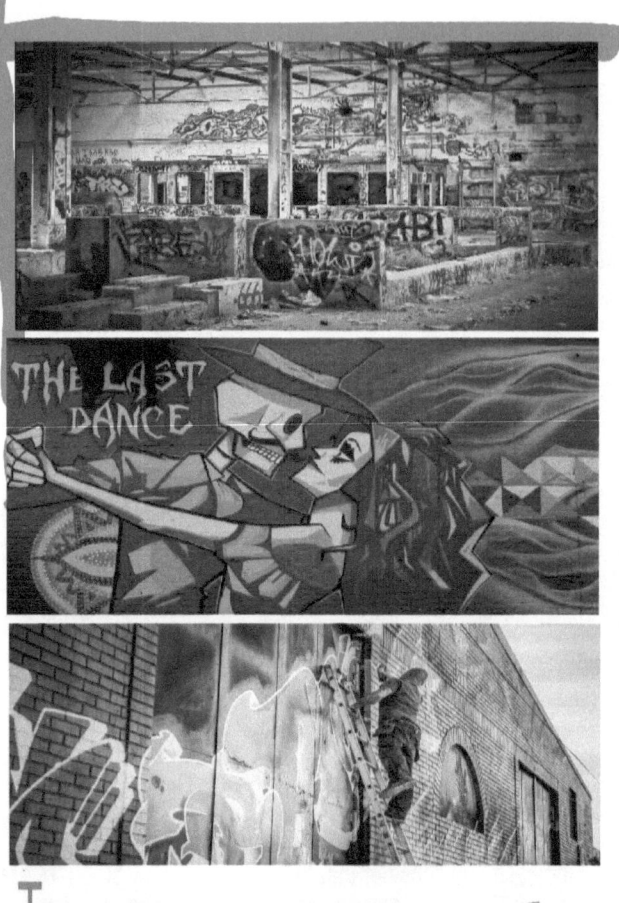

These are examples of graffiti artists around the world. There are many likewise each one knows how to expand their styles and tastes in art.

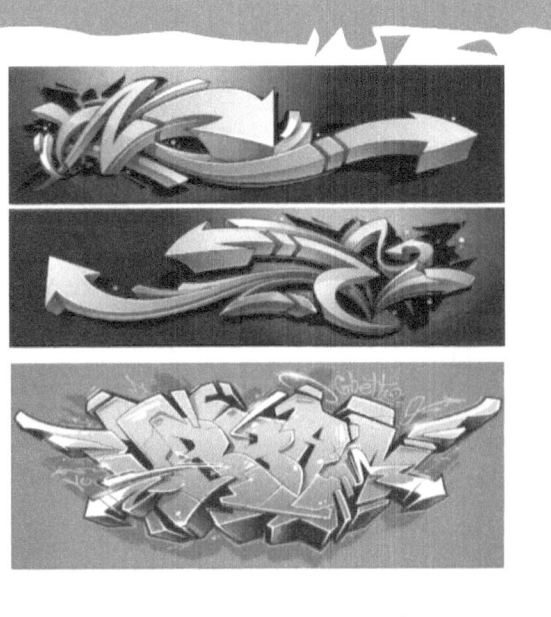

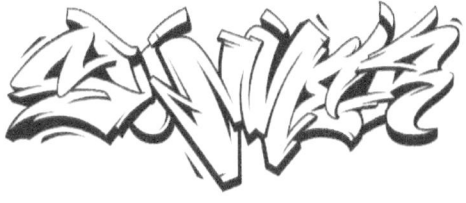

These are other typography samples (letters)
Commonly used in the world of graffiti.

Here we have a gallery of taggs
from different parts of the world.
There are also various styles for
sign.

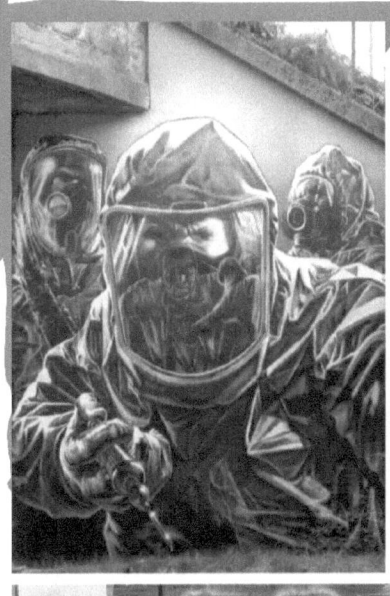
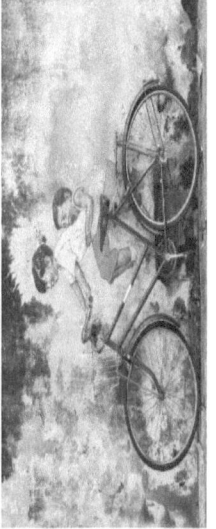
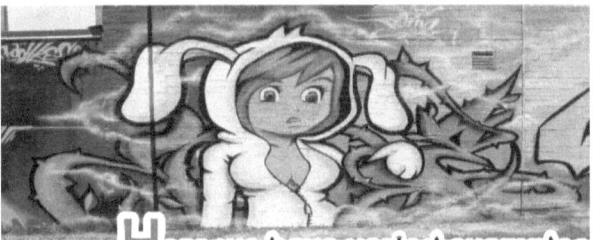

Here we have varied examples
which are classic murals that
they get to visualize around the world
often hidden, or going on
unnoticed

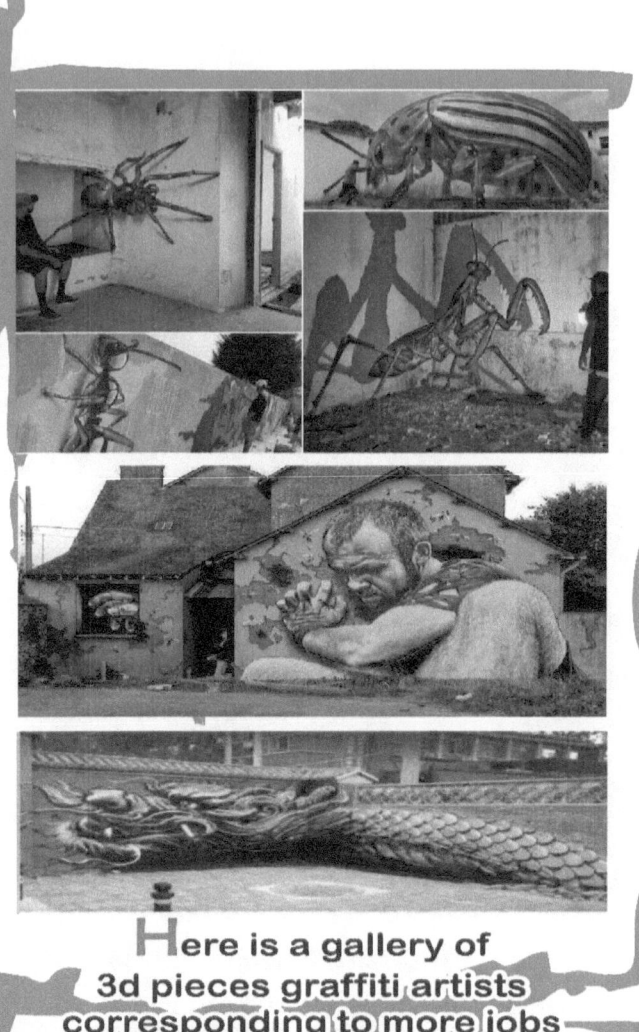

Here is a gallery of
3d pieces graffiti artists
corresponding to more jobs
complex and high quality of
capture.

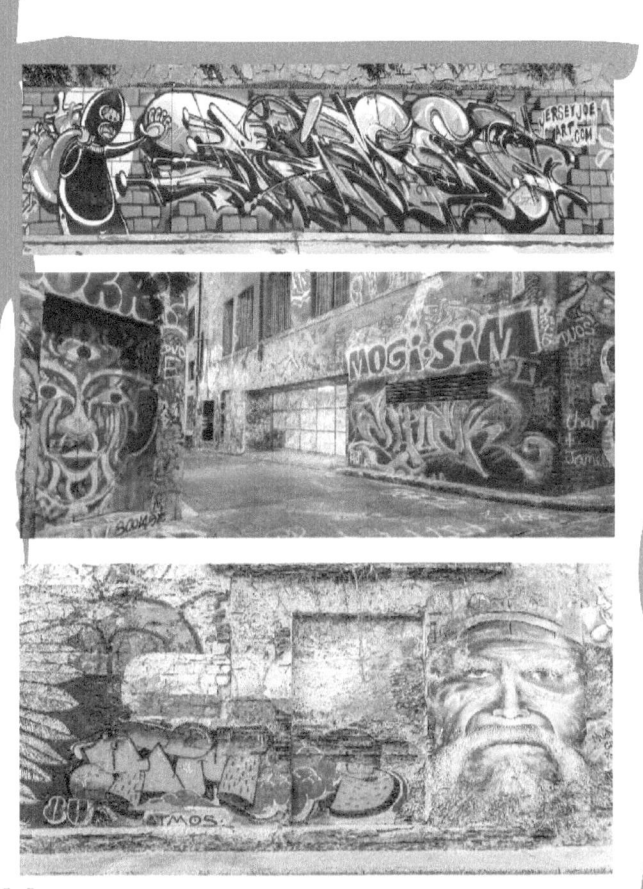

Here we have the style of letters in Bombas widely used in the world, and mainly in Mexico.

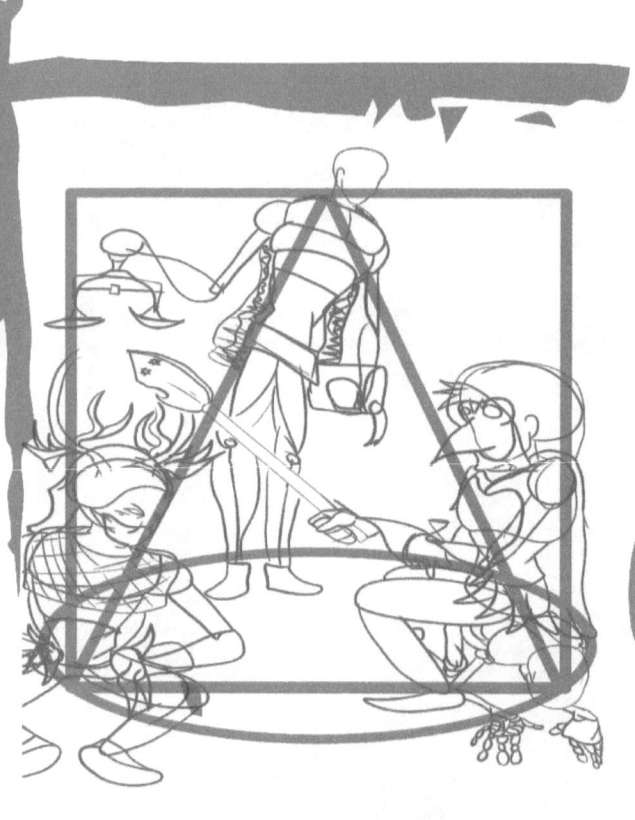

This is the sketch from which
The cover is drawn. The first
It is having an idea. The drawing of
same way as a novel,
a poem or an architectural work,
Start with a good idea.

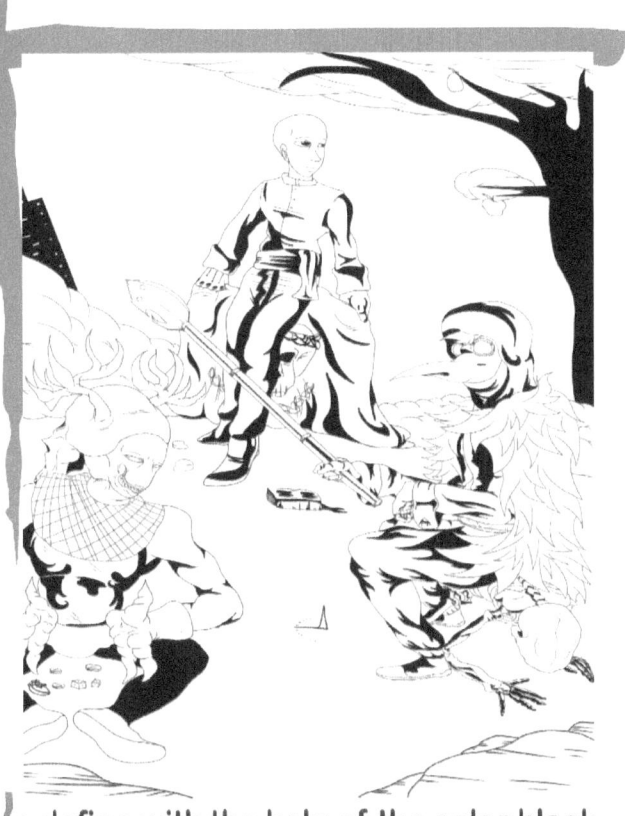

We define with the help of the color black. This graffiti was made on canvas, but in the future you can on some wall available, finish properly in the streets, near your home or mine.

47

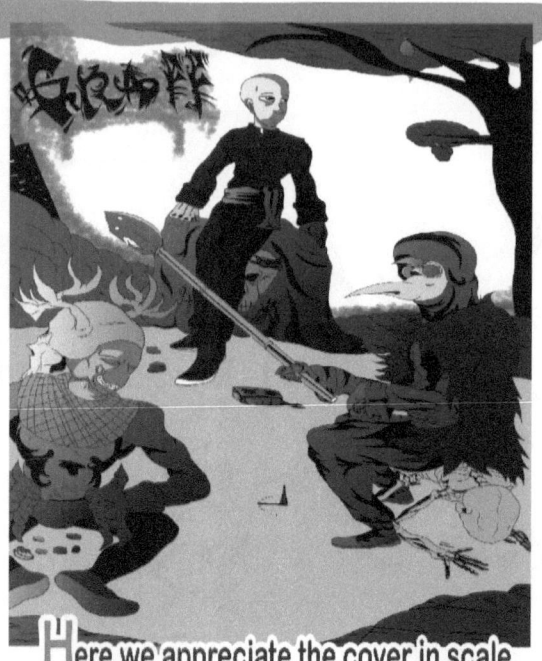

Here we appreciate the cover in scale
of gray. When we see a drawing or a
painting that is originally colored
in grayscale, we can appreciate
that we need some faint gray
and large areas of black, so
The correct cover should not look completely gray.
We must take this into account to improve
Our works.

We hope it was
Useful this guide for you.

Until next time remember that without
you would be nothing, thanks!

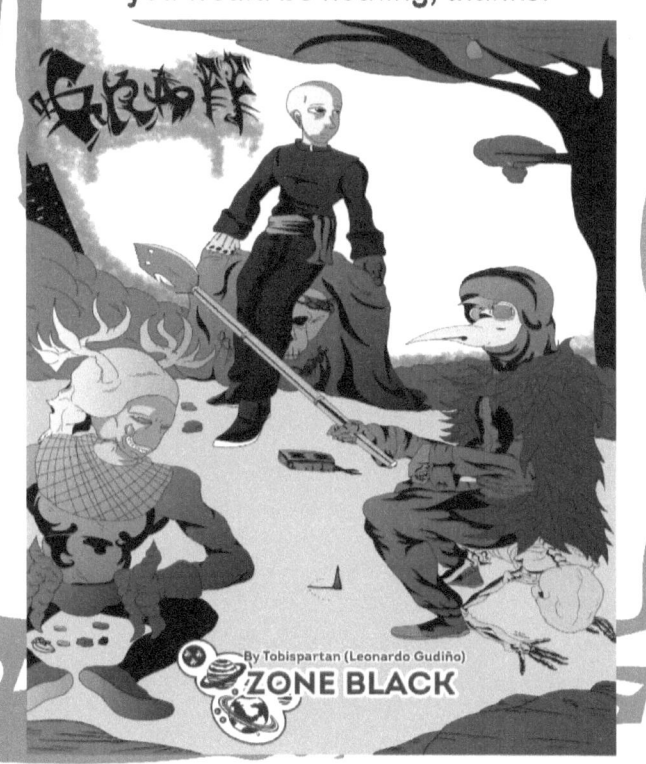

By Tobispartan (Leonardo Gudiño)

ZONE BLACK

www.ingramcontent.com/pod-product-compliance
Lightning Source LLC
Chambersburg PA
CBHW031501210526
45463CB00003B/1030